CONSERVATION OF
ENDANGERED SPECIES

SAVING THE ENDANGERED
GRAY WOLF

SHALINI SAXENA

Britannica®
Educational Publishing

IN ASSOCIATION WITH

ROSEN
 EDUCATIONAL SERVICES

Published in 2016 by Britannica Educational Publishing (a trademark of Encyclopædia Britannica, Inc.) in association with The Rosen Publishing Group, Inc.
29 East 21st Street, New York, NY 10010

Distributed exclusively by Rosen Publishing.
To see additional Britannica Educational Publishing titles, go to rosenpublishing.com.

First Edition

Britannica Educational Publishing
J.E. Luebering: Director, Core Reference Group
Mary Rose McCudden: Editor, Britannica Student Encyclopedia

Rosen Publishing
Amelie von Zumbusch: Editor
Nelson Sá: Art Director
Michael Moy: Designer
Cindy Reiman: Photography Manager
Carina Finn: Photo Researcher

Library of Congress Cataloging-in-Publication Data

Saxena, Shalini, 1982–.
  Saving the endangered gray wolf / Shalini Saxena.
    pages cm. — (Conservation of endangered species)
  Includes bibliographical references and index.
  Audience: Grades 1–4.
  ISBN 978-1-68048-250-8 (library bound : alk. paper) — ISBN 978-1-5081-0055-3 (pbk. : alk. paper) —
ISBN 978-1-68048-308-6 (6-pack : alk. paper)
  1. Gray wolf—Juvenile literature. 2. Gray wolf—Conservation—United States—Juvenile literature. I. Title.

QL737.C22S334 2015
599.773—dc23
                                                                          2015018953

Manufactured in the United States of America

Photo Credits: Cover Canon Boy/Shutterstock.com; back cover, p. 1, interior pages background stockfotoart/Shutterstock.com; p. 4 PRNewsFoto/Robin Silver - Center for Biological Diversity/AP Images; p. 5 Encyclopaedia Britannica, Inc.; p. 6 karl umbriaco/Shutterstock.com; p. 7 © iStockphoto.com/weisen007; p. 8 Barrett Hedges/National Geographic Magazines/Getty Images; p. 9 Jean-Louis Klein and Marie-Luce Hubert/Science Source; p. 10 © Michael Cummings/Moment/Getty Images; p. 11 Ronnie Howard/Shutterstock.com; p. 12 Debbie Steinhausser/Shutterstock.com; p. 13 S. J. Krasemann/Photolibrary/Getty Images; p. 14 MikeLane45/iStock/Thinkstock; p. 15 © iStockphoto.com/JudiLen; p. 16 Daniel Cox/Photodisc/Getty Images; p. 17 De Agostini/G. Dagli Orti/Getty Images; p. 18 BGSmith/Shutterstock.com; p. 19 Gary Kramer/USFWS; p. 20 Portland Press Herald/Getty Images; p. 21 © AP Images; p. 22 gdbeeler/iStock/Thinkstock; p. 23 Oleg Golovnev/Shutterstock.com; p. 24 Michael A. Smith/The LIFE Images Collection/Getty Images; p. 25 Tom Murphy/National Geographic Magazines/Getty Images; p. 26 Marcus Lindström/iStock/Thinkstock; p. 27 Jim and Jamie Dutcher/National Geographic Image Collection/Getty Images; p. 28 John Warden/Photolibrary/Getty Images; p. 29 rogertrentham/iStock/Thinkstock; cover and interior pages design elements Danomyte/Shutterstock.com (wolf graphic); David Osborn/Shutterstock.com (fur)

CONTENTS

BRAVE AND INTELLIGENT ANIMALS

When people think of wolves, they often think about the wicked wolf characters in many stories and movies. Wolves are certainly wild animals, but that does not make them evil. In fact, they are known to be brave and intelligent. Some North American Indians named their most powerful warriors after wolves. Early humans admired wolves and hunted with them in order to overtake large prey.

Wolves might look and sound frightening, but there is a lot we can learn from them.

Vocabulary

A **species** is a group of similar living things that are able to produce offspring with one another.

There are three wolf **species**. The best known is the gray wolf. It lives in North America, Europe, and Asia. The red wolf once lived throughout the southeastern United States. Now most live in captivity. The Ethiopian wolf lives in Ethiopia.

All species of wolf are in danger of dying out. This is partly because their habitats are being destroyed. People also kill wolves because they attack cattle. Today, there are many programs to protect wolves.

gray wolf, timber wolf
(*Canis lupus*)

30 cm
12 inches

Gray wolves are the largest of the three wolf species. All wolves have many similarities.

SHADES OF GRAY

Gray wolves look somewhat like dogs, though they have larger heads and bushier tails. In fact, they belong to the dog family Canidae, which includes the coyote and the jackal. However, unlike dogs, wolves are not kept as pets.

As you might guess, the gray wolf's fur is usually gray. It may also be brown, red, white, or black. The animal's legs and belly are yellowish white. Gray wolves have powerful teeth and jaws. They also have very sharp senses. The males are larger

Their sharp teeth help gray wolves attack and eat their prey.

Think About It

In the Arctic, where there is snow or ice for much of the year, gray wolves have white or light-colored fur. How do you think this helps them survive?

than the females. A male gray wolf usually weighs about 100 pounds (45 kilograms). Including the tail, it is about 6.5 feet (2 meters) long.

Gray wolves are built for traveling long distances. Their long legs, large feet, and deep, narrow chest help them stay on the move after prey. They can travel up to 30 miles (48 kilometers) in a day!

Gray wolves can run fast for short stretches of time while chasing their prey.

GRAY AREAS

There are many kinds of gray wolves. They can be found in North America, Europe, and Asia. About five kinds live in North America.

Gray wolf habitats include forests, deserts, mountains, prairies, and frozen regions. As long as they have a source of food, wolves can generally survive anywhere. In the United States, many gray wolves live in forests or wooded areas. Some gray wolves live near cities if

Thick fur helps gray wolves survive. Their paws and claws help them grip ice without slipping.

Compare and Contrast

Compare and contrast the different gray wolf habitats. What dangers might they face in each? How might each habitat help gray wolves survive?

there is enough wild prey. However, these areas also have dangers, including cars and humans.

Gray wolves can survive outside for long periods of time with little shelter. Females will stay in a den, usually a hole or burrow in a hillside, to give birth. A few weeks after wolf pups are born, they are moved outside.

Gray wolves might make their own dens, or they might use the empty dens of other animals.

PART OF THE PACK

Gray wolves are social animals. They live and travel in groups called packs. Members of a pack form strong bonds with each other. A wolf pack usually has a pair of adult wolves and their offspring. Most packs have about 6 to 10 wolves. However, some packs may have more than 20 members. A male leader and female leader, known as the alpha pair, keep order. Wolves usually mate for life.

Pack members care about each other and may even give up their lives to protect the others.

Think About It

A wolf howl can be heard for miles. How can howling help protect other wolves in the pack? In what ways might howling bring danger?

Both males and females hunt. Males usually lead the search for food. Females are in charge of raising and caring for pups, but all wolves help look after the young.

Wolf packs set up territories, or areas in which they hunt. Territories can be from 31 to more than 1,200 square miles (80 to 3,000 square kilometers). Gray wolves mark these territories with scents, barks, growls, and howls. This keeps other packs away.

Gray wolf howls can be heard from 6 to 10 miles (10 to 16 kilometers) away.

RAISED BY WOLVES

Spring usually brings the birth of gray wolf pups. Most litters have four to six pups. Pups are born blind and deaf but can see and hear after about three weeks. They live in a den for several weeks.

After about eight weeks, pups are moved outside to an area called a **rendezvous** site where they sleep and eat while adults hunt. Pack members gather at the rendezvous

By autumn, gray wolf pups can wander up to 2 or 3 miles (3.2 or 4.8 kilometers) from the rendezvous.

Vocabulary

A **rendezvous** **site is a meeting place or area.**

site during the summer. The pups learn proper wolf be-
haviors. In autumn, pups are ready to hunt and travel. By
about age one, a wolf is adult size.

After two or more years, wolves may decide to
leave the pack to look for a mate and establish a new
territory. Wolves that stay with a pack may one day become an alpha of the
group. Gray wolves can
live up to thirteen years in
the wild, but few live more
than five years. Many die
as pups.

Gray wolf pups will jump on
adult wolves' faces to get
food from them.

NATURAL PREDATORS

Gray wolves are predators, which means they kill and eat other animals for food. They eat small animals such as mice and squirrels, large animals such as deer and moose, and dead animals that they find. They will eat small amounts of vegetables or fruit.

Gray wolves normally hunt at night in groups. They travel long distances every night to find enough food to eat. Pack members often work together to outsmart large prey and find

Gray wolves will look for weaker members of a herd to attack.

Think About It

When gray wolves live in areas where there are many large prey, their packs tend to be larger. Why do you think this is?

its weaknesses. Gray wolves are able to survive days or even weeks without a meal. They can eat up to 22 pounds (10 kilograms) in one sitting to carry them through long periods with no food. Still they are at risk of starving to death in some areas.

Many gray wolves do not attack livestock, such as sheep. However, others have attacked livestock. The farmers and ranchers who own the livestock then hunt the wolves.

Gray wolves usually only kill as much as they can eat. They do not hunt for fun.

A LONG BATTLE

Although gray wolves rarely attack humans, the two have struggled to live together peacefully for centuries. Once gray wolves were the most widely spread land mammal in the world, after humans and lions. Now their numbers have dropped because of human activity. Gray wolves have few natural enemies other than humans.

Once gray wolves were all over the United States. Now they are only in certain areas, like the Rockies, in much smaller numbers.

Compare and Contrast

Humans have caused a number of animals to become at risk of dying out. In what ways is the gray wolf's story similar to other animals' stories? In what ways is it different?

Gray wolves used to live all over North America and throughout Europe and Asia. During the last few centuries, people viewed wolves as evil creatures, a danger to humans, and a threat to livestock. People poisoned, trapped, and shot wolves to protect livestock. By the 1700s, there were no more wolves in the British Isles. Nearly all disappeared from Greenland and Japan in the 1900s. By 1950, only a few hundred gray wolves were left in the United States outside of Alaska.

Some people used dogs to help them find and kill gray wolves.

OFFICIALLY ENDANGERED

Wolves keep an ecosystem strong. They rely on deer, moose, elk, bison, and other animals for their food. But those animals rely on wolves as well. Gray wolves often attack only weak or sick members of a herd. This keeps the herd population healthy.

Other animals benefit, too. Wolves leave carcasses that feed coyotes, foxes, bald eagles, and other species.

When the number of wolves in the wild decreased

Wild herds of elk become healthier after gray wolves eat their weaker members.

Vocabulary

To be endangered **means to be at risk of dying out completely.**

because of hunting, the populations of other animals also suffered. In addition, it is likely that gray wolves began attacking livestock because humans started hunting their other sources of food. The US government finally took action. Gray wolves were listed as **endangered** after the Endangered Species Act was passed in 1973. According to this law, the government must make sure that people do not hunt or harm species listed as endangered. The species' habitats are also protected.

After the US government placed the gray wolf on the endangered species list, people took action to protect them.

SANCTUARIES

A wolf sanctuary in Maine helped this gray wolf become healthy after an illness.

People have helped gray wolves by keeping them in safe places called sanctuaries. The wolves are given large spaces to roam in and meat to eat. These conservation centers often allow visitors so that people can learn about wolves and help protect them. Some wolves at a center may one day return to the wild.

These efforts have helped many wolves, including the

Compare and Contrast

Compare the lives of gray wolves in sanctuaries to those of animals in the wild. What are the pros and cons of each?

most endangered gray wolf: the Mexican gray wolf. It was once common in southwestern North America. By the 1970s, there were only five wild Mexican gray wolves. They were found and kept in captivity to protect them and allow them to breed. Today, about 300 Mexican gray wolves live in captivity.

In the late 1990s, some Mexican gray wolves were set free. Today, more than 100 of the wolves live in the wild.

This Mexican gray wolf roams around a wildlife refuge in New Mexico. It might be allowed to enter the wild one day.

THE CASE OF YELLOWSTONE PARK

Conservationists helped bring gray wolves back to Yellowstone Park after they disappeared for decades.

In certain areas, such as the Northern Rocky Mountains, conservationists introduced gray wolves from other places to help the wolf population grow. Some wolves naturally migrated to the Rockies, whereas others were brought by conservationists. This effort greatly affected Yellowstone National Park in Wyoming.

The United States made Yellowstone a national park in the late 19th century. At that time, the

Vocabulary

A **keystone species** is a species that has a very large effect on its ecosystem because of what it eats or any resources it provides.

United States was paying people to hunt gray wolves. Hunters poisoned elk carcasses and left them out for the wolves to eat. In 1926, the last two wolves in Yellowstone were killed by park rangers.

Gray wolves are a **keystone species**. When they disappeared from Yellowstone, many species in the park were also affected. The elk population grew and overgrazed, causing less plant diversity to exist there. This caused other animals, such as songbirds and beavers, to disappear. The loss of beaver ponds affected the park's water and land formations and other animal populations.

Before human settlers moved west, gray wolves could be found all over what is now Yellowstone Park.

Not everyone wanted to bring wolves back to Yellowstone. Many people signed forms to show that they supported it.

In 1995, a program was started to bring gray wolves back to Yellowstone. Wildlife workers brought about 30 gray wolves from Canada to Yellowstone. The new wolf population quickly grew. By the end of 2005, there were at least 13 gray wolf packs and 118 individual wolves living in Yellowstone National Park.

The Yellowstone ecosystem changed. Elk herds moved to areas where they could better defend themselves against wolves. This caused the plants they usually fed on to thrive. Animals, like certain birds and beavers,

Think About It

Even though gray wolves are important to Yellowstone, humans should still stay away from them. What are some ways the park can protect both wolves and human visitors?

used those plants for food and shelter. Other species, such as badgers, owls, and hawks, fed on elk carcasses that wolves left behind.

When wolves were absent, coyotes were one of the main predators in the park. They fed on ground squirrels, voles, and pocket gophers. The return of wolves helped keep both the coyote and rodent populations at healthier levels.

Gray wolves in Yellowstone keep the ecosystem in balance, which helps many different animals in the park, including beavers.

NOT OVER YET

Although gray wolf populations are recovering, they still need help. Many people who live near wolf populations in Yellowstone or areas of the Southwest, especially ranchers, worry. People still kill wolves to protect livestock. Some still trap and hunt them for sport.

People destroy wolf habitats to build homes or offices. This means wolves have smaller territories in which to hunt. They might

Gray wolf numbers have grown, but the animals need help surviving in certain areas.

Think About It

Some states, such as Michigan and Minnesota, are better about protecting wolves than other states, such as Idaho and Wyoming. Why do you think this is?

be driven to areas with humans and livestock in order to find food.

Conservation efforts can even cause problems for gray wolves. Wolves that are born in captivity cannot return to the wild because they never learned to hunt or live in packs. Wild gray wolves lost protection in some states when their population began to re-cover. When this happens, it is up to a state to protect wolves. However, some states do little to help.

Even though living in captivity has helped many wolves, these wolves often cannot survive in the wild.

HOPE FOR THE FUTURE

The gray wolf's struggle has taught us much about protecting the world's species and ecosystems. Although there are still problems, gray wolves have come a long way. There are now about 9,000 gray wolves in Alaska, 3,700 gray wolves in the Great Lakes region, and 1,700 gray wolves in the Northern Rockies.

Zoos, wildlife organizations, state governments, and other groups are still working to restore gray wolf populations across the

Gray wolves in Alaska have faced less danger from humans than wolves in other states.

Compare and Contrast

Compare the conditions that gray wolves faced in the United States in the 1950s to those they face today. Are the wolves better off now? Why or why not?

United States. Some groups have given ranchers equipment, such as better fences, that keep wolves away and cause no harm to wolves or livestock. Students can visit a local conservation center or zoo to learn more about gray wolves and share what they learn. Knowing how to protect wolves may help other endangered species in the future. The more people become involved in the conservation of gray wolves, the more they can help gray wolf populations and ecosystems.

Learning about gray wolves is an important first step in protecting them.

GLOSSARY

CAPTIVITY The state of being kept in a place without being able to leave or be free.

CARCASSES The bodies of dead animals.

CONSERVATION The protection of animals, plants, and natural resources.

DIVERSITY Having many different types of something.

ECOSYSTEM Everything living and nonliving that exists in a particular environment.

HABITATS Places where a plant or animal naturally lives or grows.

LITTERS Groups of young born to an animal at a single time.

LIVESTOCK Farm animals (such as cows and horses) that are kept and raised and used by people.

OFFSPRING The young of a person, animal, or plant.

OVERGRAZE To eat too many of an area's plants to the point of causing them not to grow.

PREY An animal hunted or killed by another animal for food.

RECOVERING Bringing back to a normal condition after a time of difficulty.

SANCTUARY A place that provides shelter or protection.

FOR MORE INFORMATION

Books

Gangemi, Alphia. *Hunting with Wolves*. New York, NY: Gareth Stevens Publishing, 2013.

Goldish, Meish. *Gray Wolves: Return to Yellowstone*. New York, NY: Bearport Publishing, 2008.

Hirsch, Rebecca E. *Gray Wolves: Howling Pack Mammals*. Minneapolis, MN: Lerner Publishing, 2015.

Llanas, Sheila Griffin. *Gray Wolves*. Minneapolis, MN: ABDO, 2013.

Shea, Adele. *Wolves in Danger*. New York, NY: Gareth Stevens Publishing, 2014.

Slade, Suzanne, and Carol Schwartz. *What If There Were No Gray Wolves?: A Book About the Temperate Forest Ecosystem*. Mankato, MN: Picture Window Books, 2011.

Websites

Because of the changing nature of Internet links, Rosen Publishing has developed an online list of websites related to the subject of this book. This site is updated regularly. Please use this link to access the list:

http://www.rosenlinks.com/CONS/Wolf

INDEX